What Ordinary Objects

Advance Praise for
What Ordinary Objects

Liz Chang's poems are brave investigations. The dark is unintentional, but attended to. The questions multiply faster than the answers. The world here is faithful to how things are. We are located in a place which is unknown, but comforting, and somehow familiar. All is fair game in Liz Chang's search. In service of her poetry, she enlists voices, including that of the French poet Claude de Burine. She installs everyday materials, accesses collage, erasure, Wikipedia, and, of course, the natural world to establish contact. *What Ordinary Objects* is a daring book, an extraordinary one. – Leonard Gontarek
  author of *Déjà vu Diner*

In her new book, *What Ordinary Objects*, Liz Chang holds several conversations at once. There is the conversation between Chang and the French poet she translates, Claude de Burine, sensitive and elegant translations that echo her own poems, making a reader feel as though she is listening in to something most private. There is the dialogue between ordinary objects and the invented, and between sensuous colors and cautious colors. These are tactile poems. They are bursting with hues and scents, filling a reader's senses. Chang does not want to miss anything in the world; she wants to discover its secrets. She wants to become and to say aloud everything, the unsaid and the impossible to know. In her translation, Chang tells us, "Language alone is the bronze that lasts." Chang's luminous poems last inside the reader's memory long after reading. – Amy Small-McKinney
  author of *Clear Moon, Frost*

Liz Chang's compelling poems explore themes like the frailty and temporality of the human body, the inevitability of death, and the responsibility of family as witness…Some of the poems express both the beauty and the entrapment of sexual desire and the need for intimacy. And throughout, Chang gifts us with her imagery—beautiful , fluid images of suspension, floating, water and the sea…Chang's poetry is riveting and ambitious.
  – Kathleen Sheeder Bonanno
  author of *Slamming Open the Door*

What Ordinary Objects

Poems & Translations
by Liz Chang

Book&Arts Press

2012

What Ordinary Objects
Poems & Translations by Liz Chang

Copyright © 2012 by Liz Chang

All rights reserved.
No part of this book may be
reproduced or transmitted in any form
or by any means, electronic or mechanical,
including photocopying, recording,
or by any information storage and retrieval system,
without permission in writing from the publisher.

Published by

Book&Arts Press
Wynnewood, PA 19096-3810
www.book-arts-press.com

Design by Jon A. Pastor
Cover Photograph by Liz Chang

Library of Congress Control Number: 2012936175

ISBN 978-0-9795861-3-2

1.0.1

This one is for Chris

Contents

i Acknowledgments
iii Author's Note

The Footfalls of the Seasons

3 Dreaming, I Was Complicit
5 We Die
7 The Acquired Knowledge of Childhood
9 The Schoolyard
11 On Brûle
13 Elegy for a Day
15 Under the Blue Light
17 The Girl Who Would

The Stone Already Remembers

23 Living in a Basement After Paradise
25 We
27 I Am Writing a Sestina for My Cat, But You Creep In
31 Jealousy
33 Divorcing Tara Donovan
35 The Waiting of the Finch
37 Portrait of the Artist Setting Feminism Back Sixty Years
39 I May Still Be Your Zelda

A Gold Bracelet Found

45 Weathering
49 Postcard to His Wife
51 It Is Late
53 Things I Thought You'd Come Back For
55 On Telling A Man By His Feet
57 By the Time I Will Have
59 Erasure/Collage Elegy

Acknowledgments

Grateful acknowledgement is given to the following literary magazines and anthologies in which some of these poems first appeared:

Poetry Ink (2009) "On Telling A Man By His Feet," (2010) "Living in a Basement After Paradise," (2011) "The Girl Who Would"

Mad Poets Review "Elegy for a Day"

Philadelphia Stories "Dreaming, I Was Complicit" and "Postcard for His Wife"

Apiary Review "Divorcing Tara Donovan" (as "Farewell to Tara Donovan"), "Erasure/Collage Elegy"

The Iowa Summer Writing Festival Anthology (2010) "Portrait of the Artist Setting Feminism Back Sixty Years"

The Adirondack Review "Under the Blue Light," "The Schoolyard," and "It is Late"

Psychic Meatloaf "Weathering"

The Breakwater Review "I May Still be Your Zelda"

The following translations and originals are published with the special permission of La Bartavelle: "Under the Blue Light," "The Schoolyard," "We," "It Is Late"

Author's Note

I think this second book is darker than my first, but that was never my intention. I do not remember a time when I was not aware of the fragility of life—even when, as a teenager, I was supposed to feel free from my own mortality. A writing mentor once said that every poem we write wrestles with the same question or, less generously, obsession. She claimed that my preoccupation was "the life behind things." She pegged me after reading only four of my early poems.

I think this question/obsession arises from the fact that I've always had a pretty good memory. Maybe I see the life behind things because I remember subtle connections that other people might forget. For instance, "The Acquired Knowledge of Childhood" draws on the autobiographical fact that I pushed a red crayon up my nose when I was four and had to go to the emergency room to get it removed. Some corner of my brain says that this action made sense at the time—when I think back to that moment, I am convinced that I did it because I wanted to make red a part of me. It was someone's favorite color on the television show I was watching.

So let's stipulate that this is not a book about death—it's really not. Mainly, this book is about the life behind things embodied in the objects, memories, and people around us. In fact, the poem that lends its line to the title came out of a dream I had. What began as a terrible burden—literally, plucking boxes off a shelf to determine who was next in line to die as some sort of perverse Death-internship—began to grow into something almost comforting and necessary. A theme that comes up a lot in these pages is alienation, and I mean that in a literal way: there are several places where I've attempted to work in "moon" words as an homage to my grandfather's involvement in the early space program. However, the other side of alienation is intimacy; many of these poems are also about intimacy: real or perceived, attained or lost.

The poet I chose to translate, Claude de Burine, writes a lot about dying from love. Perhaps I need to translate her work because the most salient characteristic for me is her preoccupation with the life that runs through everything, silently partnering with mortality. She writes on an emotional plane, which extends outward infinitely in every direction, encompassing various scenes and locations from every age. In intertwining my translations of her work with my own poems, I hope that these pieces will speak back-and-forth to each other in conversation across time and space and language.

When I was actively working on these translations (in 2008), I could not find a lot of biographical material on her. She is famous inside France, but her work has garnered minimal international attention. The few details I did find indicated that she was in ailing health and that she had traveled to Paris to get treatment for what was seen as her final illness. Several years later, I found an obituary that mentioned that she'd passed away from a pulmonary embolism in 2005. Only two people were present at her interment. At the time when I was translating her, I always thought of her as a living poet, and in fact, I believe the words she left behind transcend her own lifetime. What an incredible personal loss it is for me to realize that she is no longer with us. There is so much I wish I could have asked her.

Notes on the Poems

The short biography of Tara Donovan at the beginning of "Divorcing Tara Donovan" draws upon the Wikipedia entry under her name. It was accessed on July 14, 2011.

The online interview that was the basis for "Erasure/Collage Elegy" first appeared as "Speak, Memory" and was conducted by Maya Singer for Style.com with the Mullavey sisters (Laura and Kate), who created the LA-based fashion line Rodarte. It serves as the erasure basis of my poem. I then collaged in the emails. This interview was accessed on December 18, 2008 at 12:55 PM.

The Footfalls of the Seasons

Dreaming, I Was Complicit

You stood over
my shoulder, goading me
one hand cupped
on my waist, as I
decided who would die

with each new shoebox
opened, some clue
to their identities inside.
A bird's nest, ashes,
small keys the size
and crouch of regurgitated
mouse skeletons.
What ordinary objects
stood for whole lives.

The last box was fit
for children's shoes
with a purple, incidental
print on the outside.
I opened the top,
relieved to find
my grandmother's
autumn-colored flats.

Somewhere,
she must be shuffling
barefoot inside
her fading isolation,
searching for an end.

On meurt

On meurt de son enfance,
De ses boiseries,
De ses arbres aux muscles forts,
De sa terre qui bouge
Sous le pas des saisons,
Plus sûrement encore
Que de l'amour.

Mais on meurt d'un amour
Qui vient à la nuit tombée
Quand le soir a brodé son manteau
D'étoiles messagères
Que ses mains sont vêtues
Du cuir doux des rencontres
Que ses paroles ouvrent la salle
Où paraissent dormir
Ceux qui nous attendent.

We die
Claude de Burine
published online in *Poésie Maintenant* (2006)

We die from childhood,
from our wainscoting,
from our strong-muscled trees,
from our land that stirs
under the footfalls of the seasons,
more surely still
than from love.

But we die from a love
that comes in the dark of night
when evening has embroidered his cloak
with messenger-stars
and his hands are covered
with the soft leather of meetings
so his words open the room
where they seem to be sleeping,
the ones who wait for us.

The Acquired Knowledge of Childhood

I wanted to know the body of red.
—a child only knowing
body and breath, tumbling against
the tops of her knees, sloshing
inhalations through her nose

and back again. I sent red there
and it felt familiar
a sidewalk pointed toward home.
(Red wants to be carried
because it has stubby legs.)

Barkburned inner wrists and ankles
grasp to aid red's climb
farther into my head.
It cleared my eyes
so I saw everything:

white stings,
yellow feels lean
brittle, perched at home
inside the dryer vent. But green
becomes frantic: blueberries

eaten with the skins still on.
Green cries unfinished or gone
too soon. Green whispers Manny
and seed pods shuddering
to Box's Air on G on vinyl.

La cour

La cour de l'école est déserte, le cerisier noir.
Les cahiers sont rangés.
On a tué le dernier oiseau.
Dans l'île, la barque est tirée,
La musique éteinte.
Je t'attendais. Je mangeais tes pas.
J'étais l'attente. J'étais tes pas. J'étais la faim.

Tu ne passeras plus.
Je n'attendrais pas. J'attendrai.
Je serai la faim qui brûle.

The Schoolyard
Claude de Burine
from *Le Passager* (1993)

The schoolyard is deserted, the black cherry tree.
The books are all put away.
Someone has killed the last bird.
On the island, a boat is drawn up,
The music turned off.
I waited for you. I ate your path.
I became waiting. I was your path. I was hunger.

You will not come this way again.
I would not wait for you. I will wait.
I will be the hunger that burns.

On Brûle
a reflection on de Burine's "La Cour" ("The Schoolyard")

On the day after the weekend
returning to the beating heart of our childhoods,
we found the ghost tree
crumbling in the yard, a stubborn
yet half-living urn
still clinging to the body of the stone wall.

We found the classrooms hastily
inkwashed with freckles of black ash,
the desktops' expectant faces
sudsy and filmed.

Someone had cut around his footsteps,
the melted map of his flight.
Virginal carpet mocked
the safety of nap-squares
drawn up: an unanswerable
wool archipelago.

Children will devour
the details we proffer.

I do not forget.
I become your witness.
I became your story:
We walked through painted doors
into hallway smelling
slightly sweet in April
of wool and dust.

A tide of scorched air filled our lungs,
and embers, glittering fireflies.

I am ashamed
to say out loud
that I am lost.

Elegy for a Day

If we are past seasons of being woken
to happiness, remembering
the slosh of the horse beneath
our thighs and the growl
of equine moorings gliding
past crest and fallen landforms

then let me find the secret joy etched
in penciled plans, encircled by expansive white,
flowing past their structure to eek out hours
of familial bliss and grass
to witness our affiliation running
together, as if free.

If he has passed, let me imagine
him always astride the careful pony.
Once more, father, trespass
and let me be there to shovel out
the avalanche of your laughter.

Sous la lumière bleue

Sous la lumière bleue de l'enfance,
Là où le parquet ciré
Sent le miel et le bleuet
Où l'œillet blanc garde son goût
De vanille et de poivre,
Tu avais la voix
Qui lançait les trains, les navires,
Faisait glisser la barque,
Les péniches au ventre noir
Comme l'exil,
Filer les canards gris
Quand les roseaux étaient des couteaux de nacre
Entre les mains du gel.

Quand venait la nuit
Ta voix allumait les feux des bateaux
Qui vont vers les îles
Et tu partais,
Me laissais les yeux vides de l'absence.

Under the Blue Light
Claude de Burine
from *Le Passager* (1993)

Under the blue light of childhood,
there where the waxed floor
smells of honey and cornflower
where the white carnation retains its taste
of vanilla and pepper,
your voice could
launch trains, ships,
make boats glide from their slips—
the barges with their black bellies
like exile—
release grey ducks
when the reeds were pearly knives
in the hands of frost.

When night came
your voice stoked the fires of the boats
that go toward the islands
and you left,
leaving me behind, the empty eyes of absence.

The Girl Who Would
with love, for CMS

I am the girl who learned to float
helicopter seedpods from your brother
and who walked behind you,
wishing to sweep
giant, brush-cleaner forsythia
against my cheeks
to know I was home.

I have been craving
grasscloth wallpaper, with its tiny
irregular knots printing our skin
and the hill that we would roll down
again, again
catching bits of Rapunzel's
hair in our teeth.

I am that girl, still
in the shared driveway
dragging my fingertips
along wood-look ribs
of the station wagon or throwing
found fossils against the ground,
hoping to unlock further secrets

fool's gold. In the end,
I am the girl who would look up
stage four lung cancer on tar-and-feather
websites that mitigate every prognosis
and research clinical trials. Today,

my hopes for you have lesions.
I wish to give you more time.

The doorframe into our shared past
throbs in my head until I can feel
only the cold slate floor
despairing at the sweet,
tangy smell that settled
as tiny orange scales, into grout
in your father's breath, into
eyelashes over every surface.

The Stone Already Remembers

Living in a Basement After Paradise

If I speak against the dead, I must skirt
your longing for the slip of mortal mantle

from your shoulders. You bow your heads
and go through, sorting

cracked and twisted settings, broken plates to be
placed back into the cabinet after a portion of

rice and fish. So if we found you'd gone,
there would be no crumbs, just closed drawers

and the lace tablecloth draped,
hanging lopsided, as hastily as I laid it

for a picnic two years ago, smiling.
Boxes stand sealed, canopic jars

of evidence preserved between pages of tax timetables,
we were other people once,

receptacles of your past beautiful life
as you two bear mummification

in this the pharaoh's tomb.

Nous

Nous ne sommes peut-être qu'un rêve,
Un mouvement des épaules de Dieu
Dans son sommeil aux yeux ouverts.

Tu viens de si loin,
Tu restes, si près de nous, pour nous vivre
Que tu es la barque au clair de lune
Que l'on ramène
Quand la mer a le goût de l'amour.

Etre avec Toi,
La minute première
Où déjà le caillou se souvient,
Où la pâquerette est ivre d'être l'enfant
Qui danse sous le soleil.

Les réverbères à Paris
Sont toujours ces clochards pensifs
Qui promènent leur ombre.

Et dessous, le moineau raconte.

Ton silence: ce froid soudain.
Reçu comme une dépêche.

We
Claude de Burine
from *Le Passager* (1993)

Perhaps we are only a dream,
A shrug of God's shoulders
In his restless sleep.

You come from so far,
Resting close to us, for us to live with
You as the moonlit boat
Drawn back
When the sea tastes of love.

To be with
You the first minute,
When the stone already remembers,
When the daisy is drunk from being the child
Who dances in the sunlight.

The streetlamps of Paris
Are those pensive homeless
Out walking their darkness.

And below, the sparrow speaks.

Your silence: that sudden cold.
Received like a Tweet.

I Am Writing a Sestina for My Cat, But You Creep In

Ears like construction paper (taut) bounce back,
their surface rubbed into rag texture.
Collar reflects light onto the floor
she chases her own golden glint like foil-paper
skittering across the parquet. Turning,
she slides into crown molding, flattening an ear in royal dismay.

She plays off the white-pawed tangle, such dismay,
arches and twists her birch-striped back
so it brushes against everything, claiming it, turns
her chin into the edges of my hand's worn texture
until I feel my eight folds crisply, origami paper.
Before I can dwell on this, a pan clatters to the floor.

She skitters across the honey floorboards
her wide-legged gait projecting her dismay
at this apartment, animated so easily, flapping paper
in a draft. Silence. Stillness. She turns back
to the sill, staring into the street's broken texture.
She is purposeful and reluctant to return.

I wanted to chide the leaves for turning
their bruised shades after you left. I felt the floor
lurch and knew the same textured
flaw Sylvia sprouted at twenty—her dismay
at having lived—on her cheek, grown back
an ominous wax seal on white rag paper,

I caught that scar through her pages.
I still think of how you loved this porch, you'd turn
to look at me, looking at your back.
It's winter now: the season to make love on the floor
and absolve ourselves. But thawing, my dismay
uncovers lash-marks left by your callous texture.

The cat stalks the apartment for your rough texture,
some clue of you: finds a chapped newspaper
you brought in, left beside the bed. You were dismayed
by my ignorance of the news, at my turning
inwards and tossing the world on the floor.
It's a cheap lesson that I want you to take back.

So the cat arches back her dimpled stomach's texture,
stroking across the floor. Rustling the paper,
she offers me distraction, to turn away from my dismay.

Jalousie

Pas elle,
La triste,
l'endeuillée,
Mais moi,
la mendiante aux sabots d'or,
la voleuse
dans le clair de lune du coeur.
Regarde mon visage
Et regarde mon ventre,
Je cède et je me hâte
vers les grands roseaux noirs
qui lièrent nos corps,
J'aurai des souvenirs
qui me briseront la gorge,
Quand mes mains inconnues
déferleront vers toi.

Jealousy
Claude de Burine
from *Poésie 1* (1979)

Not her,
the sad one,
the mourning woman,
but me,
the wanderer in golden *sabots*,
the she-thief
in the light of the heart's moon.
Look at my face
and my belly,
I recede and hasten
towards the great black reeds
that bound our bodies.
I will have those memories
tearing at my throat
when my unfamiliar hands
surge toward you
like the tide coming in.

Divorcing Tara Donovan
    The artist Tara Donovan uses office materials to create large-scale sculptures of ecological scenes.

In terms of infinity, when
we lost him, thousands
of molded tape dispensers
shone, scales on a giant fish-back,
ebbing from East River docks
and I wished your dribbling thump
thump of his clenched body in the box
down the stairs had not subsumed

my longing for a headstone. I followed
your eyebrows' embrace,
the ponderous expression, with a fat
white eraser cradled in my fingers,
rending bits of slackened skin
with each sure stroke.
We watched the broadcasts
(another school shooting).

We winterized our windows with
paperclips, pencil shavings
forming a topographic map
of we should have known,
of closing up
of battening down of
is it too late now? We don't discuss
but commemorate

a whisper of grass
the last one we witnessed

outside the Brooklyn Museum of Art
growing haughtily
toward the solar possibilities
of incandescent streetlamp,
that lived on as gestural purple
at your temple when

I stopped to draw you.
I might have known
how you would exit
a flourish of dramatic appreciation
a *tour de force*, only
the closed chamber of the cab
echoing through the street.
I might have drowned

in a continent of ten thousand
discarded, translucent cups
trapping single-servings
of oxygen underneath.

The Waiting of the Finch

We were not to mourn her, but
I found this tucked
among the Tupperware
after she died:

here, she is processing angles
with her eyes. He is
an aspen branch, and
Antoinette is lovely,

her keel jutting out
from the folds
of her wrapdress. Behind her,
the plates will soon be cleared.

I see her now, pitched forward,
considering her descent.
A vain woman, as we all are, who
dusts off her femininity

each morning carefully
reshaping Waterford hair.
She who set the table
with paper plates!

He promises her something
with this confidence
(protection) misdirected,
grinning his gibbous smile
toward their companions,
who blink at the camera's
manifestation: bloated, wispy

cloud edges in an already grey sky.

If she blushed at this image,
her serenity split open,
I want to ask her if she'd known
when she wove her home

the kind of life that lay ahead of her
the deep cone
the weft from treachery,
the yawning edge
of his warp
and wanderlust.
The universe of this photograph
reveals nothing, just the unyielding

gristle of love, brief twinge of an alarm call.
She asked me once how to change
my baby sister and at six I knew
she had misunderstood but

I didn't have the heart
to correct her. I am ashamed
to remember my disgust
at the end of her life

when her sepia-tones leaked out,
staining our pillowcases.
Her diagnosis, perch
and path determined
she decided to be cremated
and fell into flight.

Portrait of the Artist Setting Feminism Back Sixty Years

I do not have a house, but if I did, you could
come unbidden and I would like to serve you
little tarts on color-coordinated napkins
the size of your palm.
If I had one wish, it would be
for strings of pearls to plant
as perennials
and then world peace.
I would invite all the former despots
for amaretto cocktails.
My grandmère only drank men's drinks,
but I have an elevated disgust factor
and am supposed to be coded for conservatism—
as if there's a straight line,
or one that curves slightly right,
between eviscerated guts and gays.
(Snakes and snails and puppy dog tails,
they say.) I say there's nothing nicer
than emerging unscathed
from Norman Bates' shower.
I purr warnings and terms of endearment:
poet-tess so it rhymes with Loch Ness.
My eyelashes become elevated
in importance when
I'm writing.
I will not wait
for age to catch my pedicured toe

and if you suggest grace,
I will thaw my Miss Deepfreeze 1953
brilliance and petrify you
where you stand.
You twist into a juniper tree
that I can be certain to revive
with the proper recipe of a 24-carat locket
folded into a paperweight.
In the meantime, I can drink infusions.
I only mourn the poor ladybugs
that will curl up like eyelashes
and perish in such rough company
...and then the poor puppies
and the feminists who might always lament
their severed tails.

I May Still Be Your Zelda

I think you love my half-life
each time it folds in upon itself
and unleashes a new, rough face,
the automatic compactor

of memory inside me, crushing everything—
appropriated elegies still ache,
purpling in my poet brain.
How I cling to you when I wake from

brittle nightmares with the push
of the coaster car pulling into the locks once more.
Yanked back to land atop the Ferris wheel
at the fireman's fair, I did not know

one place could contain so much suffering.
Our life, a study in simultaneous
contrast: two colors stand next to each other
their similarities magnified.

You see the violet in my red and I see the blue
in your brown confidence, certainty
suspended inside your words
like salt in saline. It permeates

the shelter of the car
that planetarium
of want. I remember
the Carolina sky with you

hole-punched into confetti and
breathe out. We paint the nursery
lemon verbena and contemplate
the lavender wash of the empty fields

of the sanitarium and surrender:
how lucky we will be
to have our very own Scottie, mascot
of the normal life everyone lusts after.

A Gold Bracelet Found

Weathering
for two voices during a natural disaster

When he arrives, he will see me
as I intend. Olympian.
    Already the heat drains from the crater
sprawled on the bed,
coy in my garters
        that had cradled the mountain of his
           shoulders,
and lace, as he loves me.
    the slope of his masculine hips.

I pull the sheets
closer,
    in around me, hoping,

Where do mistresses come from?

cocooned, my gaze floats
to the window,
    I am Mexican chocolate.
picture Dan as he fords back
        through the city
    I am red. I am cayenne.
    to his other life.
Taste me, Daniel, you will burn.

And you eat
The whole city seems awake
    every bite
and still, as I was,

                   when he slipped out the door.
a taste for me on your swollen lips.

This is a familiar moment.

*I crack the chain,
the housewife from across the hall surfaces*

Sirens cut through my isolation
        in front of me, pale as a fish.
Opening and closing her thin mouth,
singing my sadness.
              she tries to dislodge words.

But the room is full of heaviness
and something is wrong.
     Remembering the sweetness
that once seduced you
and now   (I never let him see me
stir, send him away with the
postcard-image:

I feel possessed with wanting
to tell her
        me, languid and still
I cry at how you love me.
        luxuriant in the love we'd made.)

I am ashamed, thinking
the neighbors will hear

my loneliness.

    You're scalded and never sated.
I want them only to cringe
at how bodily he loves me.

I read her curlers and desperation:
They look at me through the lens
    it is barely light,
of the side-view mirror, distorted,
knowing my life teeters on the edge
    with the white loneliness of a new day to face,
the fires are coming—something
they will never understand,
but desire.

Postcard to His Wife

How long he kept your name for himself—
the sea reaches for the smooth breast
of the shore and turns away.

Now the ocean comes back to me in all my poems.
Here the wind whirls your name into crescendo. Where
we lay awake in sandy arsenals

he talked about moving inland. I must have laughed.
Now the pipers pick over the man of war
washed of his armor and shuddering plum dye,

all that is left of this cup of new Narcissus
who was a fool to have settled for the pond when
he could have run into the sea, embracing

hundreds of mollusk admirers who might
die and rot and still call after him. They pine
for their first love down to chiseled bone.

I wished I'd been a monument when
I heard him say, "I've met someone." Instead,
I read and re-read the indictment of the tide

slapping the staid shore, wishing to grow gills
and drown kissing air. Then you could cut along my ribs
and pry me open, find flecks of mercury winking
to know that he had flown.

Il est tard

Il est tard
Le froid vient vite.
Les chemins se creusent.
L'Automne n'a pas donné d'ordres
Mais la lumière baisse.

L'étain va reprendre ses pensées.
Le cuivre, ses voyages au long cours.
Le marron sa destinée d'oursin des campagnes.

Les meubles attendent.
Les fenêtres, les portes, se méfient, se ferment.

Comment te rejoindre
S'il n'y a pas les roses,
Les routes pour aller pieds nus?
Te parler
Près d'un canal qui gèlera bientôt?
Sous la clarté brune des bistrots à Paris
Où la bière est capitaine du navire?

Nous avions les feuilles, avant,
Les fleurs, les silences.
Mais la main ne s'est pas tendue
Et tout s'éteint
Comme un bracelet d'or
Trouvé dans les parcs

Le veilleur de nuit
Commence ses rondes.

It is Late
Claude de Burine
from *Le Passager* (1993)

It is late.
Cold comes quickly.
The paths fold in on themselves.
Autumn hasn't given the order yet
but the light fades.

Pewter will take back its thoughts.
Copper, its long travels.
The chestnut, its destiny as a displaced, spiny urchin.

The furniture waits.
The windows, the doors, close themselves, wary.

How to find you again
if there aren't any roses,
any roads to follow, barefoot?
To speak to you
by a canal that will be icy soon?
Under the brown light of Parisian bistros
where beer is captain of the ship?

We had the leaves, before,
the flowers, the silences.
But your hand is not offered
and the light goes out of everything
like a gold bracelet
found in the park.

The night-watchman
begins his rounds.

Things I Thought You'd Come Back For

Your photographs, their pocks and dents, it seems you've given and taken them back before. The serious set of your features under the airman's insignia. The jersey of your favorite team with the last name you gave me stenciled across my shoulders. The print of my couch's lines on our torsos. The hopeful white of your shirt when you came to see me before telling her. The sand of your scalp. The crunch of your everyman boots on the ice of my marble steps. The ankleboots I pulled on to walk, finally confident you wouldn't go without me. The growl of the metal teeth on your zipped-up windows that you "unlocked" to get your cigarettes. The gesture of your lips pressed to the same stick, the way you offered it to me on my turn. Your prickled sigh as you brushed my bare stomach beneath the hem of my shirt. The swing of your hips. The rafts of your lips. The slate look in your eyes when you knew you'd given too much. The shimmering heat in the stillness of the air when I didn't chase you. The noise I couldn't hear in the silence when my heart broke. The soundtrack that overtook me; the CD I'd meant to burn for you. The sad story of the boy who had lost his father, only to get him back and find out how much he wasn't. The mother who always knit acclaim and pain. The wrench that left Cheshire cat grins. The perfect blue of the Pennsylvania sky and the treestand like Peter's hideaway. The narrow porch where I stared at roofing supplies in gallon buckets while my father called my name and called and called. The blips of your voice that came through the bad reception: sweetie… hang… love. The burdened lean of the mattress. The cracked tape in the banquette when I told the story for the first time. The ice in the glass that couldn't move because it was so tired.

On Telling a Man By His Feet

B's feet fit the oyster-shell of my palm,
rocking into sleep on the tide. Sloughing off
worn, crusted barnacles, exposing
pilings, he was reborn in layers.
I held my heart in my hand.

The next twisted his toes into tree knots,
slated digits digging their own channels
into hard ground, sprouting
small hairs, setting down roots.
Curled around gravestones
they bury their faces in
the sifting sand, at home
in the company of the dead
and dying.

My love has autonomous feet, fairytale feet—
now marred by rocking back and forth,
leaning down to kiss me, soles exposed
and matched to his, cradled as
he brushes the sea through my hair,
leading me down, away from the headstones,
rubbing printed names from my skin.

Mais quand j'aurais

Mais quand j'aurai fermé les yeux
Que vous serez sous les violettes
Ou les ronces comme moi
Que les nuages au-dessus de nous
Se feront se déferont comme nous,
Qui parlera pour nous?
Qui dira: «Toi, tes yeux,
Sont la couleur de la rêverie
Et des jeunes ardoises
Au printemps des pluies

Et toi: ta peau
Est la grive qui chante,
Tes mains sont ma chaleur
Et la fièvre de l'été
Qui porte ton nom».

Le temps va où il veut
Pose son habit de jonquilles
Et d'eau où il veut,
Nous n'avons rien
Qu'une aile de papillon qui sèche
Contre les vitres de la nuit.
Nous ne sommes rien qu'une poussière
Sous les lèvres avides du vent.
Seul le langage
Est le bronze qui dure.

By The Time I Will Have
Claude de Burine
from *L'Arbre aux Oiseaux* (1996)

By the time I will have closed my eyes
and you are under the violets
or the brambles like me,
the clouds above us
will be made and unmade like us,
who will speak for us?
Who will say, "You, your eyes
are the color of a daydream
and newly lain slate
in the spring rain.

And you: your skin
is the thrush that sings,
your hands are my warmth
and summer's fever
which bears your name."

Time wanders on,
wearing its clothes of daffodils
and water where it wants,
we don't have anything
but the wing of a butterfly that dries
against night's windows.
We are nothing but dust
on the eager lips of the wind.
Language alone
is the bronze that lasts.

Erasure/Collage Elegy
from an online interview and emails received between April 24 and May 5

        It may be a long way,
    but on a good day
it's where
                the work gets done; analyzed
                    It's a curious thing to discover
     everything
and as we know
His discharge date
keeps changing.

Morgan is still in the hospital
                amid all that
     mild
expressive
doctors are not very clear
          heels   side-by-side   and humming
sometimes with their explanations of
words that are
similar in meaning (such as "cat" for "dog")
or similar in sounds
("foot" for "phone")
                But that was exactly
                    to us   what we already knew
As of now, it might be this Wednesday
Everyone flocks together.

Once you get outside
                the scenes popping up

He's still a bit disoriented, especially at night,
And occasionally
during the day
            probably the only
errors made are sometimes
                    secret
because he
just hasn't mentioned anything.
hasn't mentioned any more
of the hallucinations
Recently
            you   realized
last night, driving—   late, and the
whole city
            transformed.

            We passed
Constellations of what keeps you in

    I think we've been really lucky
that we're
a city of misfits
                close-knit
        we have such a strong connection
  We grew up   but it's still sometimes difficult
                        not trying to be
invented. And
            Yesterday, after a few days of declining

mental
insularity, becomes   clear
he will be
heading directly to hospice care.
                    Hubble discovered that the universe was
                                                    out there, with
              the cancer all over his lungs as well as in his lymph nodes
                                        one month before
. Just that one month, when there was nothing else—only

              freeway and a garden, like us.
No one knows what this means in regards to the future.

 Everyone always says to us
    concentrate quietly: God,
maybe we don't need
to come back   together, and
    to breathe
              to
figure out what kind of cells there are
    we happened to be
          the memories, color, and that—
   maybe there are some things you ought to say out loud—   together.

About the Author

This is Liz Chang's second book of poetry from Book&Arts Press. Her work has been included in several anthologies and literary magazines, and her translations have recently appeared in The Adirondack Review.

She is 2012 Montgomery County Poet Laureate and Assistant Professor of English at Delaware County Community College. She received her MFA from Vermont College of Fine Arts and lives with her fiancé and their two cats *en les environs* of Philadelphia.

Colophon

The body of *What Ordinary Objects* is set in several styles and weights of Adobe Minion, created by master calligrapher and type designer Robert Slimbach. Released in several versions between 1990 and 2000, Minion is inspired by classical, old style typefaces of the late Renaissance, a period of elegant, beautiful, and highly readable type designs. Crisp and open, it politely defers to the text, and allows itself to serve as a vehicle without adding its own statement.

Titles and headings are set in Agfa Rotis Semi Serif, a unique hybrid with characteristics of both serif and sans-serif faces. It is one member of a family of four fonts designed by Otl Aicher, and named after the village in the Allgäu where he has lived since 1972.

The Book&Arts Press logo is set in Linotype Zapfino, a tour-de-force of type design, a truly calligraphic face with a vast number of variants for most characters, including decorative ("swash") characters like the ampersand ('&') in our logo. Its creator, Hermann Zapf, is universally regarded as one of the greatest calligraphers and type designers of all time. Zapfino has the unique ability to function with equal facility in the most formal and the most informal settings.

Also by Liz Chang
from Book&Arts Press

Provenance: Poems by Liz Chang

Liz Chang's poems remind us that ordinary life is only apparently so, as it offers up disjunctions and provocations, undercurrents of violence, and moments of fierce sensuousness to someone willing to observe them with a forthright gaze. These are the poems of a poet fully awake to what goes on within her and around her, and she renders all of it, through restraint and consistently fresh metaphors, as macabre but not threatening, necessitating a measure of courage, and ultimately familiar.

> – Leslie Ullman
> author of *Slow Work Through Sand*

"We do not remember days, we remember moments," the great Italian poet, Cesare Pavese once wrote in his diary. And this is precisely Liz Chang's sophisticated and heart rending performance here. In one poem she writes, "I tear out the delicate core at the belly / of the orange, and think of the moment / I exposed myself to you." The lines not only give us a complex psychological scene but resonate with other moments in this extraordinary book where a "train flashes past like the angriest storm," and where being "exposed," as she says in "Rambla dels Ocells," is both a danger and a means of recovery, piecemeal of what Pavese calls a "secret reality coming to bloom." From the personal to the familial to the social, Chang makes her moments resonate into a wondrous and redemptive whole.

> – Richard Jackson
> author of *Resonance*

www.ingramcontent.com/pod-product-compliance
Lightning Source LLC
Chambersburg PA
CBHW032209040426
42449CB00005B/509